Made in the USA
Las Vegas, NV
09 August 2024

93574800R00063